The Forward Book
of Poetry 1997

FORWARD PUBLISHING
LONDON

First published in Great Britain by
Forward Publishing · 5 Great Pulteney Street · London W1R 4LD
in association with
Faber and Faber · 3 Queen Square · London WC1N 3AU

ISBN 0 571 19000 6 (paperback)

Compilation copyright © Forward Publishing 1996
For copyright on individual poems see acknowledgements page 7
Foreword copyright © Alan Jenkins 1996
Front cover illustration by Marion Deuchars

Typesetting by Graphic Ideas
Karen House · 1-11 Baches Street · London N1 6DL

Printed by Redwood Books Ltd.
Kennet House · Kennet Way · Trowbridge · Wilts. BA14 8RN

A CIP catalogue reference for this book
is available at the British Library.

To Molly

Preface

THIS IS THE FIFTH FORWARD BOOK OF POETRY. The poems in this book have been chosen by the judges from entries to the Forward Poetry Prizes and represent some of the best poetry written in the English language and published in Britain and Ireland in the last year.

As is the tradition, this anthology is published on National Poetry Day, now in its third year: a day of poetic celebration throughout the nation. This year we hope that every child in school will get the opportunity to read, write or learn a poem on the day. And thanks to the help and support of the Worldwide Fund for Nature, the official charity for the event, every school has been equipped with teachers' packs and teaching materials to promote poetry for a new generation of enthusiasts.

Our prizes and anthology are designed for the older reader and, we hope, provide a divining guide to contemporary poetry for the enormous numbers of new fans to the art.

As always, we at the Forward Poetry Trust would like to thank the many people who helped make all this possible: Simon Forrester at the Worldwide Fund for Nature, Gordon Kerr at Waterstones, Jeffery Tolman at Tolman Cunard and everyone at the BBC, the Poetry Society, Colman Getty and Forward Publishing.

And of course our thanks to the ever hardworking judges who sifted through a record number of entries to the prizes and chose this wonderful anthology.

William Sieghart

Foreword

PERSONALLY SPEAKING, it's been a bad year for poetry. Since last autumn, two friends, two poets, Gavin Ewart and Joseph Brodsky, radically different in their aims and achievements, have died. Both, in their radically different ways, were important to my sense of what poetry was about, and important to numerous others besides. I haven't wanted, personally, to write much, or even cared that much. Perhaps, until they weren't there, I hadn't realised the extent to which their example underwrote what I thought I was doing – something very different from what they did. (Admire and do otherwise, that's how we cope with older poets: older poets, anyway, with the talent and dedication of those two.) Now they weren't there. And just what was poetry about?

Then the entries for the Forward Prizes started coming in, and I began to make my way through them. And it hasn't been a bad year for poetry at all; it's been a perfectly good year. Which is to say that dozens – maybe hundreds – of volumes of poetry have been published, and hundreds – maybe thousands – of poems, in a multitude of magazines, big and small. Not all of this poetry is good; some of it is not much more than a gesture towards an idea of poetry, of the poem as gentle therapy, as honest recording of experience or as well-meaning anecdote, in serviceable prose, only prose that doesn't go to the end of the page. I and all my fellow judges, Penelope Fitzgerald, Michele Roberts, Alastair Niven and Sean O'Brien, longed to be surprised by an individual rhythm, by an ungainsayable strength of feeling, by a voice that knew words as certain good; by poetry that had been uttered because there was no other option. This book is the sum of our surprises, the record of our discovery – individual and collective – that all these, and sometimes all of them together, are to be found in the poetry now being written in English.

The point of the Forward Prizes is to bring the best of that poetry before the wider public it deserves, and our shortlisted books are those we especially wanted, individually, collectively, democratically, in the mysterious way these things happen, to welcome. The entry for Best Collection was impossibly strong. Given a shortlist twice the length of our permitted five, new collections by Ciaran Carson, Les Murray, Penelope Shuttle and Craig Raine might well have appeared on it.

The five we did choose look stronger by the minute. Our short shortlist for best First Collection, on the other hand, reflects the fact that only four books, among a plethora of entries, had sufficiently caught and held our attention. (Young poets, notation is not enough; cleverness is not enough.)

Wherever there are prizes there are lucky poets who carry cheques away (and as I write we do not know who they will be), but the beauty of the Forward is this spacious anthology, where all the poems that moved or delighted us are to be found. The accidents of publishing history threw up some anomalies. One part of Seamus Heaney's sombrely brilliant sequence about internecine strife, 'Mycenae Lookout', was on the Best Poem shortlist last year, under that title; but the sequence is plainly (intricately) the best thing in his collection, *The Spirit Level*, so to represent him by anything else would have seemed wrong. Another sequence, 'The Prophetic Book', by Craig Raine, had already been published in its entirety before it reappeared in his collection *Clay. Whereabouts Unknown*, so he is represented by a much shorter but (I think) exquisite and wholly characteristic poem. The Best First Collection list reverses the man-to-woman ratio of the Best Collections, as it did last year: another accident. It is presumably no accident that the sharp-eyed editors of the magazines *The North* and *The Rialto* were able to muster so many impressive entries for the Best Poem.

I can't mention everything and everyone I'd like to here, and in any case the Forward Prizes exist to throw (in the words of Carol Ann Duffy, my predecessor as Chair) their 'glamorous and searching' spotlight on an art that continues to speak eloquently for itself, in and out of the glare. A final word of thanks, then, to my fellow-judges, to William Sieghart of Forward Publishing, and to Margot Weale of Colman Getty who brings the books, the poems and the judges together so painlessly. This book is for them to be proud of, and others to enjoy.

Alan Jenkins

Acknowledgements

Fergus Allen · A Time for Blushing · *Who Goes There?* · Faber and Faber

Moniza Alvi · An Unknown Girl · *A Bowl of Warm Air* · Oxford
    University Press

John Ash · In Khorkum · Poetry News Review

John Ashbery · The Problem of Anxiety · *Can You Hear, Bird* · Carcanet

Patricia Beer · Art History · London Review of Books

Charles Boyle · White City · Sheds · *Paleface* · Faber and Faber

Eleanor Brown · The Lads · *Maiden Speech* · Bloodaxe Books

Ron Butlin · Advertisement for a Scottish Servant · *Histories of Desire* ·
    Bloodaxe Books

Ciaran Carson · Alibi · *Opera Et Cetera* · Gallery Books/Bloodaxe Books

Kate Clanchy · Slattern · Recognition · *Slattern* · Chatto

Harry Clifton · Reductio · Poetry Review

David Constantine · Bombscare · Poetry Review

Julia Copus · The Art of Interpretation · Miss Havisham's Letter ·
    The Shuttered Eye · Bloodaxe Books

Robert Crawford · Chaps · *Masculinity* · Cape

Kevin Crossley-Holland · The Language of Yes · *The Language of Yes*
    Enitharmon

Allen Curnow · Pacific 1945–1995 · London Review of Books

Alan Dixon · A Fearsome Sister · *Transports* · Redbeck Press

Maura Dooley · The Message · The North

Theo Dorgan · The Match Down the Park · *Rosa Mundi* · Salmon Publishing

Mark Doty · New Dog · *Atlantis* · Cape

Lauris Edmond · The Pace of Change · *In Position* · Bloodaxe Books

Steve Ellis · Gardeners' Question Time · Poetry Review

U A Fanthorpe · Atlas · Collateral Damage · *Safe as Houses* · Peterloo Poets

John Fuller · 'Prudence dans l'Eau' · The Garden · *Stones and Fires* · Chatto

Adèle Geras · The Suitor · The Rialto no 34

David Hart · This is the Vessel · Oxford Poetry/winner of Lincolnshire
    Festival Poetry Competition

Seamus Heaney · MYCENAE LOOKOUT · *The Spirit Level* · Faber and Faber

W N Herbert · FEATHERHOOD · SMIRR · *Cabaret McGonagall* · Bloodaxe Books

John Hughes · 1812 · *The Devil Himself* · Gallery Books

Kathleen Jamie · THE GRADUATES · Times Literary Supplement

August Kleinzahler · SNOW IN NORTH JERSEY · London Review of Books

Michael Laskey · THE VISITATION · The North

Marion Lomax · DIVIDED WE STAND · *Raiding the Borders* · Bloodaxe Books

E A Markham · STAND-IN · *Misapprehensions* · Anvil Press

Adrian Mitchell · MOVING POEM · *Blue Coffee: Poems 1985-1996* · Bloodaxe Books

Paul Muldoon · THE HUG · Times Literary Supplement

Les Murray · THE EARLY DARK · The Rialto

Sharon Olds · MRS KRIKORIAN · *The Wellspring* · Cape

Alice Oswald · WOMAN IN A MUSTARD FIELD · MY NEIGHBOUR, MRS KERSEY ·
        The Thing in the Gap-Stone Stile · Oxford University Press

Ruth Padel · A DRINK IN THE NEW PIAZZA · London Review of Books

M R Peacocke · GOOSE HYMN · *Selves* · Peterloo Poets

Mario Petrucci · FOETAL DREAM · TOP OUR ROAD, BOTTOM OUR ROAD ·
        Shrapnel and Sheets · Headland

Ian Pople · THE SAME CONDEMNATION · FELLOW TRAVELLERS · *The Glass
        Enclosure* · Arc Publications

Peter Porter · A SECRET LIFE · The Rialto no 34

Tom Pow · LEONA · *Red Letter Day* · Bloodaxe Books

Craig Raine · HEAVEN ON EARTH · *Clay. Whereabouts Unknown* · Penguin

Christopher Reid · TWO DOGS ON A PUB ROOF · *Expanded Universes* ·
        Faber and Faber

Mark Roper · RED HANDED · The North

Carol Rumens · BEST CHINA SKY · *Best China Sky* · Bloodaxe Books

Lawrence Sail · ANOTHER PARTING · *Building into Air* · Bloodaxe Books

Penelope Shuttle · EIGHT FROG DREAMS · *Building a City for Jamie* ·
        Oxford University Press

George Szirtes · THE LUKÁCS BATHS · *Selected Poems 1976-1996* ·
        Oxford University Press

Andrew Waterman · DORA, DICK, NIP AND FLUFF · *The End of the Pier Show* ·
 Carcanet

Kit Wright · THE ALL-PURPOSE COUNTRY & WESTERN SELF–PITY SONG ·
 Poetry Review

Glyn Wright · THE MARY ELLENS · *Could Have Been Funny* · Spike

Peter Wyton · AT THE END OF THE KILLING LINE · Smiths Knoll 10

Contents

Shortlisted Poems from the Best Collection Prize

Charles Boyle · Paleface   14

U A Fanthorpe · Safe as Houses   16

John Fuller · Stones & Fires   18

Seamus Heaney · The Spirit Level   22

W N Herbert · Cabaret McGonagall   30

Shortlisted Poems from the Best First Collection Prize

Kate Clanchy · Slattern   36

Julia Copus · The Shuttered Eye   38

Alice Oswald · The Thing in the Gap-Stone Stile   40

Ian Pople · The Glass Enclosure   42

Shortlisted Poems from the Best Individual Poems Prize

Patricia Beer · Art History   46

David Constantine · Bombscare   48

Maura Dooley · The Message   50

Kathleen Jamie · The Graduates   51

Les Murray · The Early Dark   53

Other Poems 1996

Fergus Allen · A Time for Blushing   56

Moniza Alvi · An Unknown Girl   57

John Ash · In Khorkum   59

John Ashbery · The Problem of Anxiety   62

Eleanor Brown · The Lads   63

Ron Butlin · Advertisement for a Scottish Servant   65

Ciaran Carson · Alibi   66

Harry Clifton · Reductio   68

Robert Crawford · Chaps   70

Kevin Crossley-Holland · The Language of Yes   72

Allen Curnow · PACIFIC 1945-1995   73

Alan Dixon · A FEARSOME SISTER   76

Theo Dorgan · THE MATCH DOWN THE PARK   77

Mark Doty · NEW DOG   80

Lauris Edmond · THE PACE OF CHANGE   83

Steve Ellis · GARDENERS' QUESTION TIME   84

Adèle Geras · THE SUITOR   85

David Hart · THIS IS THE VESSEL   87

John Hughes · 1812   88

August Kleinzahler · SNOW IN NORTH JERSEY   89

Michael Laskey · THE VISITATION   91

Marion Lomax · DIVIDED WE STAND   92

E A Markham · STAND-IN   93

Adrian Mitchell · MOVING POEM   94

Paul Muldoon · THE HUG   95

Sharon Olds · MRS KRIKORIAN   97

Ruth Padel · A DRINK IN THE NEW PIAZZA   99

M R Peacocke · GOOSE HYMN   103

Mario Petrucci · FOETAL DREAM · TOP OUR ROAD, BOTTOM OUR ROAD   104

Peter Porter · A SECRET LIFE   106

Tom Pow · LEONA   108

Craig Raine · HEAVEN ON EARTH   110

Christopher Reid · TWO DOGS ON A PUB ROOF   111

Mark Roper · RED HANDED   114

Carol Rumens · BEST CHINA SKY   115

Lawrence Sail · ANOTHER PARTING   116

Penelope Shuttle · EIGHT FROG DREAMS   117

George Szirtes · THE LUKÁCS BATHS   120

Andrew Waterman · DORA, DICK, NIP AND FLUFF   122

Glyn Wright · THE MARY ELLENS   125

Kit Wright · THE ALL–PURPOSE COUNTRY & WESTERN SELF-PITY SONG   126

Peter Wyton · AT THE END OF THE KILLING LINE   128

The Best Collection Poems

Charles Boyle

White City

They will be selling our clothes, I know that now.
Our biscuit tins. Our boxing gloves.
Our rolls of surplus wallpaper.
Our tools and gardening equipment, hammers
and rusted sickles and the rake with bent tines.
Our model soldiers.
Our wireless set, on which we listened
to the national anthem and the racing results from Catterick.
Our loved ones and anniversaries
and twilit landscapes in their rickety frames; our books,
bookshelves, light-bulbs even, our watches
that stopped on our wrists.

They will have laid them all out
in rows or piles on groundsheets or trestle tables
or in the backs of hatchback cars.
It will be early in the morning
on the day of our Lord, the sky too will look blotched,
stained, used and abused, a wind out of it
rapidly losing patience. And not
that we'll need them or care a damn who owns them,
but small chemical reactions
we might another day ignore will make it imperative
we buy them back, haggling a little
until the price is right.

SHEDS

The way weeds and stiff grasses have reclaimed the yard,
the way the tracks lead frankly nowhere;
the dry rust, the continuous mockery
of insects, of birds; the way the toolsheds
could still be nothing but toolsheds
even without their tools, with their corners smelling of shame
and their little piles of filth . . .

Exhaustion, waste, relief
at being one again with nature –
and still a kind of reckless belief
that just one more day, another hour of light
would have seen it through.

U A Fanthorpe

ATLAS

There is a kind of love called maintenance,
Which stores the WD40 and knows when to use it;

Which checks the insurance, and doesn't forget
The milkman; which remembers to plant bulbs;

Which answers letters; which knows the way
The money goes; which deals with dentists

And Road Fund Tax and meeting trains,
And postcards to the lonely; which upholds

The permanently ricketty elaborate
Structures of living; which is Atlas.

And maintenance is the sensible side of love,
Which knows what time and weather are doing
To my brickwork; insulates my faulty wiring;
Laughs at my dryrotten jokes; remembers
My need for gloss and grouting; which keeps
My suspect edifice upright in air,
As Atlas did the sky.

COLLATERAL DAMAGE

The minor diplomat who brings terms for a ceasefire
Enters through a side-door, in the small hours,
Wearing a belted raincoat.

The children have become bold. At the first siren
They cried, and ran for their mothers.
Now they are worldly-wise,

They clamour to watch dogfights above the house,
They prefer under-the-kitchen-table to the shelter,
They play fighting games

Of reading the paper by bomblight,
Pretending to be the enemy. These children
Are no longer safe.

They have learned rash and contrary for ever. Come soon,
O minor diplomat in the belted raincoat, come
To capitulate. For the children have ack-ack nerves,
And a landmine has fallen next door.

Under the reservoir, under the wind-figured water,
Are the walls, the church, the houses,
The small human things,

That in drought rise up gaunt and dripping,
And it was once Mardale, both is and is not Mardale,
But is still there,

Like the diplomat, and the crazy fearless children
Who progress through their proper stages, and the churchbells
With their nightly riddles,

And the diplomat, and the children still running
Away from shelter, into the path of the bomb.

John Fuller

'PRUDENCE DANS L'EAU'

Far from being a warning,
Today's newspaper horoscope
Is simply a tender description
Of this aquarelle you enact
As if by a maître of 1919

For whom the maillot, beyond
Its masquerading as a garment,
Becomes the tracing of a line
Negotiating a containment
Of convalescent blue.

You may picture the sea
As a requirement of masses:
Here, the caution of shoulders
A shade of biscuit against
A disintegrating wall of wave.

There, the wide wash of azure
With its pucker of cobalt
And unsettling flung creams.
And further, just off-centre,
And teacherly red tick of a sail.

It's not that you're happy to become this picture.
You're happy for once to be yourself,
Cradled in water that moves forever
Over the stones and fishes of the morning,
Beneath the stones and fires of night.

THE GARDEN

For my father

Considering that the world needs to be born
Endlessly out of our looking at it, it's no wonder that
We retire here for that purpose in our brief time.

Mappers and model-makers, traffickers
In language's unreliable schedules, all our
Journeying is a nostalgia for this.

The garden bears our traces and becomes
Through them the model of a mind which so
Defines itself: a part, and yet apart.

The world may grow here. All that is left outside
Is unimaginable, all within
So like itself that there is nothing else.

Blossom is rumoured. The mind also prepares
Its own best growth, pruning just beyond
The bud. Though summer is already past.

Leaves that would fly have lately fallen. Lifted
Once in wind, they have now become detached,
Ready to drift. And autumn, too, is gone.

Those purer spirits whose undeliberate music
Also creates a more or less habitual space
Have turned their retreat into a coded return.

These pebbled paths lead only to a point
Which shows where they have come from and that now
To continue is a figure not a journey.

Those walls were built no higher than they need be
And where they join give reasons for joining. Where not,
Is a hinge never still enough to cease to be one.

For to enter is always possible, as it is
To leave, though to do neither is at last
As much a relief as both were ridiculous.

If others care to overlook these long
Endeavours, let them, for after all we are
Contented merely with corroboration.

The solemnest face caught staring in would be
Your own. The reason that it never is
Seems like the reason for almost everything.

We are, possibly, posed this riddle early
In life: which is the likeliest of mirrors,
The face that reflects the world, or another face?

The last is not easily admitted, the first
The one we know. It is a grief that placed
Together they only do what mirrors do.

Reflections of reflections, it is said,
Are a symbol of all desire. And lead nowhere
But endlessly and shallow into themselves.

To see oneself in the garden is the final
Privilege, the last illusion like
The glittering letters in a burning leaf.

To be an image of the thing already
Containing you is surely a fine prospect,
As the fruit is an eager portrait of the tree.

And being so requires the greatest detachment,
Function of the philosopher's particular passion
To locate beauty beyond its short-lived shapes.

The garden, therefore, is a signal comfort
To those who fear that belonging is an illusion
Like longing itself, like the desire for desire.

For though it takes no pleasure in itself,
The garden is beautiful while you are in it,
And having once been you are always there.

Seamus Heaney

Mycenae Lookout

The ox is on my tongue
>   Aeschylus, *Agamemnon*

1 *The Watchman's War*

Some people wept, and not for sorrow – joy
That the king had armed and upped and sailed for Troy,
But inside me like struck sound in a gong
That killing-fest, the life-warp and world-wrong
It brought to pass, still augured and endured.
I'd dream of blood in bright webs in a ford,
Of bodies raining down like tattered meat
On top of me asleep – and me the lookout
The queen's command had posted and forgotten,
The blind spot her farsightedness relied on.
And then the ox would lurch against the gong
And deaden it and I would feel my tongue
Like the dropped gangplank of a cattle truck,
Trampled and rattled, running piss and muck,
All swimmy-trembly as the lick of fire,
A victory beacon in the abattoir . . .
Next thing then I would waken at a loss,
For all the world a sheepdog stretched in grass,
Exposed to what I knew, still honour-bound
To concentrate attention out beyond
The city and the border, on that line
Where the blaze would leap the hills when Troy had fallen.

My sentry work was fate, a home to go to,
An in-between-times that I had to row through
Year after year: when the mist would start
To lift off fields and inlets, when morning light
Would open like the grain of light being split,
Day in, day out, I'd come alive again,

Silent and sunned as an esker on a plain,
Up on my elbows, gazing, biding time
In my outpost on the roof . . . What was to come
Out of that ten years' wait that was the war
Flawed the black mirror of my frozen stare.
If a god of justice had reached down from heaven
For a strong beam to hang his scale-pans on
He would have found me tensed and ready-made.
I balanced between destiny and dread
And saw it coming, clouds bloodshot with the red
Of victory fires, the raw wound of that dawn
Igniting and erupting, bearing down
Like lava on a fleeing population . . .
Up on my elbows, head back, shutting out
The agony of Clytemnestra's love-shout
That rose through the palace like the yell of troops
Hurled by King Agamemnon from the ships.

2 *Cassandra*
No such thing
as innocent
bystanding.

Her soiled vest,
her little breasts,
her clipped, devast-

ated, scabbed
punk head,
the char-eyed

famine gawk –
she looked
camp-fucked

and simple.
People
could feel

a missed
trueness in them
focus,

a homecoming
in her dropped-wing,
half-calculating

bewilderment.
No such thing
as innocent.

Old King Cock-
of-the-Walk
was back,

King Kill-
the-Child-
and-Take-

What-Comes,
King Agamem-
non's drum-

balled, old buck's
stride was back.
And then her Greek

words came,
a lamb
at lambing time,

bleat of clair-
voyant dread,
the gene-hammer

and tread
of the roused god.
And a result-

ant shock desire
in bystanders
to do it to her

there and then.
Little rent
cunt of their guilt:

in she went
to the knife
to the killer wife,

to the net over
her and her slaver,
the Troy reaver,

saying, 'A wipe
of the sponge,
that's it.

The shadow-hinge
swings unpredict-
ably and the light's

blanked out.'

3 *His Dawn Vision*
Cities of grass. Fort walls. The dumbstruck palace.
I'd come to with the night wind on my face,

Agog, alert again, but far, far less

Focused on victory than I should have been –
Still isolated in my old disdain
Of claques who always needed to be seen

And heard as the true Argives. Mouth athletes,
Quoting the oracle and quoting dates,
Petitioning, accusing, taking votes.

No element that should have carried weight
Out of the grievous distance would translate.
Our war stalled in the pre-articulate.

The little violets' heads bowed on their stems,
The pre-dawn gossamers, all dew and scrim
And star-lace, it was more through them

I felt the beating of the huge time-wound
We lived inside. My soul wept in my hand
When I would touch them, my whole being rained

Down on myself, I saw cities of grass,
Valleys of longing, tombs, a wind-swept brightness,
And far-off, in a hilly, ominous place,

Small crowds of people watching as a man
Jumped a fresh earth-wall and another ran
Amorously, it seemed, to strike him down.

    4 *The Nights*
    They both needed to talk,
    pretending what they needed
    was my advice. Behind backs
    each one of them confided
    it was sexual overload
    every time they did it –

and indeed from the beginning
(a child could have hardly missed it)
their real life was the bed.

The king should have been told,
but who was there to tell him
if not myself? I willed them
to cease and break the hold
of my cross-purposed silence
but still kept on, all smiles
to Aegisthus every morning,
much favoured and self-loathing.
The roof was like an eardrum.

The ox's tons of dumb
inertia stood, head down
and motionless as a herm.
Atlas, watchmen's patron,
would come into my mind,
the only other one
up at all hours, ox-bowed
under his yoke of cloud
out there at the world's end.

The loft-floor where the gods
and goddesses took lovers
and made out endlessly
successfully, those thuds
and moans through the cloud cover
were wholly on his shoulders.
Sometimes I thought of us
apotheosized to boulders
called Aphrodite's Pillars.

High and low in those days
hit their stride together.
When the captains in the horse

felt Helen's hand caress
its wooden boards and belly
they nearly rode each other.
But in the end Troy's mothers
bore their brunt in alley,
bloodied cot and bed.
The war put all men mad,
horned, horsed or roof-posted,
the boasting and the bested.

My own mind was a bull-pen
where horned King Agamemnon
had stamped his weight in gold.
But when hills broke into flame
and the queen wailed on and came,
it was the king I sold.
I moved beyond bad faith:
for his bullion bars, his bonus
was a rope-net and a blood-bath.
And the peace had come upon us.

5 *His Reverie of Water*
At Troy, at Athens, what I most clearly
see and nearly smell
is the fresh water.

A filled bath, still unentered
and unstained, waiting behind housewalls
that the far cries of the butchered on the plain

keep dying into, until the hero comes
surging in incomprehensibly
to be attended to and be alone,

stripped to the skin, blood-plastered, moaning
and rocking, splashing, dozing off,
accommodated as if he were a stranger.

And the well at Athens too.
Or rather that old lifeline leading up
and down from the Acropolis

to the well itself, a set of timber steps
slatted in between the sheer cliff face
and a free-standing, covering spur of rock,

secret staircase the defenders knew
and the invaders found, where what was to be
Greek met Greek,

the ladder of the future
and the past, besieger and besieged,
the treadmill of assault

turned waterwheel, the rungs of stealth
and habit all the one
bare foot extended, searching.

And then this ladder of our own that ran
deep into a well-shaft being sunk
in broad daylight, men puddling at the source

through tawny mud, then coming back up
deeper in themselves for having been there,
like discharged soldiers testing the safe ground,

finders, keepers, seers of fresh water
in the bountiful round mouths of iron pumps
and gushing taps.

for Cynthia and Dmitri Hadzi

W N Herbert

FEATHERHOOD
(for Debbie)

1

God speaks in sic undeemis weys
that maist o whit he seys
gaes maunderin awa
in pirrs an pirlies lyk
a speugie soomin thru a hedge,

or thi soond o an ice-cream van
prinklin uts notes thru a gloamin estate
in Stranraer,
in thi middle o Januar:

ut seems ut maun be meagrims till
He talks ti you in pain
an the meisslin awa o pain,
in solace and
uts meisslin awa.

2

This is thi wey Eh didnae ken
why thi flaffin flicht
o three grey wullie-wagtails
straicht
in frunt o ma car
filld me wi mair nor fricht

undeemis: extraordinary; *maundering*: sounding indistinctly; *pirrs an pirlies*: gentle breaths and small things; *speugie*: sparrow; *soomin*: swimming; *prinklin*: bubbling; *meagrims*: absurd notions; *meisslin*: wasting imperceptibly; *flaffin*: a fluttering of the wings.

until
parkd in Castle Douglas
Eh thocht o the computer's
photie o wir ain three eggs
abstractit fae yir boady
an fertilised
by IVF:

that tho yirdit in
yir willin wame
came loose
an flew awa.

   3
An kennan this repleyed
thae ithir flee's-wing instants,
nearly stills:

o starin thru a screen intil
thi ocean o yir kelder
lyk a submariner
lukean fur the sonar ding
o wir twa-munth dochtir's
foetal hert;

o sittan in
thi doctir's oaffice
hearan hoo an acronym –
a D & C – wad dae
tae waash awa
hir kebbit pearl

yirdit: earthed; *flee's wing*: very small or short; *kelder*: womb; *kebbit*:
stillborn.

an lukean oot thi windie
at a white plastic bag
risin past oor
second storey,
a flinricken escapin.

    4

Here wiz thi sentence, then:
thi three, ma pearlie, and
wan mair simple daith,
his reid refusal tae be held –
gin ut wiz a he –
past mair nor a week o wir kennan:

mebbe ut wiz
a refusal tae be kent
lyk God's refusal tae prevent
thon previous collision
arrehvin in thi Haugh o Urr
atween meh car
an a jenny-wren:

sae sma a plosive
set this up
by silencin that sang,
sae haurd tae ken
God means yi as
His punctuaishun.

flinricken: a weak person, very thin cloth, a mere rag.

5

Sae licht thi lives that laive us
oor griefs maun growe insteed;
thi anely wean
a man can cairry's
absence inniz heid.

But leese me oan thi lea-laik-gair
that spelt me oot this speech,
thi sma hills o thi Stewartry
sae saftly preach
Eh nearly nivir heard yir nemm
i thi burr o ilka bee;

but ken noo that ut is your breist
Eh'm liggin oan tae listen.
Ut is your braith
that blaws thi feathirs o thi wurds
by me and awa.

leese me oan: an expression of preference; *lea-laik-gair*: the place where
two hills join together and form a kind of bosom; *burr*: a whirring noise
as made in the throat in pronouncing the letter 'r'; *liggin*: lying.

Smirr

The leaves flick past the windows of the train
like feeding swifts: they're scooping up small mouth-
fuls of the midge-like autumn, fleeing south
with the train's hot wake: their feathers are small rain.
'Serein' they could say, where I'm passing through,
then just a sound could link rain with the leaves'
symptom, of being sere. But who deceives
themselves such rhyming leaps knit seasons now?
Some alchemist would get the point at once;
why I, against the leaves' example, try
migrating to my cold roots like a dunce.
Thicker than needles sticking to a fir,
Winter is stitching mists of words with chance,
like smears of myrrh, like our small rain, our smirr.

The Best First Collection Poems

Kate Clanchy

SLATTERN

I leave myself about, slatternly,
bits of me, and times I liked:
I let them go on lying where
they fall, crumple, if they will.
I know fine how to make them walk
and breathe again. Sometimes at night,
or on the train, I dream I'm dancing,
or lying in someone's arms who says
he loves my eyes in French, and again
and again I am walking up your road,
that first time, bidden and wanted,
the blossom on the trees, light,
light and buoyant. *Pull yourself
together*, they say, quite rightly,
but she is stubborn, that girl,
that hopeful one, still walking.

RECOGNITION

Either my sight is getting worse,
or everyone looks like somebody else.
A trick of the light, perhaps, or shadows

in this dark bar with its fancy candles,
but I think the girl in hippy sandals
could turn, and in a spin of bangles,

be a girl I know but somehow younger,
her before I even knew her.
Or the skinny boy in the aran jumper,

hair in the nape of his neck like a feather,
could puff out smoke, be my first lover
pulling me, laughing, into the shower:

as if no one I knew had ever got older,
haircuts, glasses, or just wandered further
than I could follow, chose to bother;

as if through sheer short-sightedness,
I could recover, rewrite losses,
sift through face on face-like faces,

make one focus, crystallise,
pull towards me, recognise,
see themselves, once more, in my blue eyes.

Julia Copus

THE ART OF INTERPRETATION

A plain wood table, the obligatory
vase of flowers, the writer's head bent low
over his work. At the far end, a window.

Open. Apart from this there is little
to help us with the story: the room is left
deliberately bare, inviting us

to speculate. Consider, for instance,
the window as eye. Is it looking out
or looking in? Notice, too, the dark, plum

sheen of the nib; and the pen, not poised
but resting, heavy, on the page. Unused.
Do you see how the artist plays the light

off against the shade? The candle, also,
is misleading: I advise you to ignore
the warmth of its glow. Drop the temperature

a little. Allow your eyes to wander
over the shadows, where the details are:
the clearly-labelled absinthe flask, half full,

half empty; the sweeping lines of the words
in the open letter, just visible
under the lifeless curl of his fingers.

Now turn up the volume of background noise,
the pub's detritus in the street outside.
Bring it level with the window. Then cut.

Miss Havisham's Letter

Darling, there is nothing between us that cannot be
restored. So much remains of the good times: did I tell you

how, on the eve of our day, while in my under-garments,
I leaned over and felt the full weight of my breasts

in my own hands! And such pleasures have been replaced
by other pleasures – a kind of wisdom: my eye knows

the very corner of my eye, and my mouth has learned
to use its various muscles to full effect –

When my girl comes with food I pull a perfect scowl
but I do not refuse the tasteless sops she brings:

how else shall I sustain myself! Darling, the dress
outgrew me long ago. I hear it sometimes

cracking in its paper where the silkworms
shift and slide. It is trying to make a life for itself.

And my small night table is shaping an effigy
of you; it sags with all the candles I have burned.

Pray God that you will be here soon; the furniture
is weary, my darling, of the names I am forever

fingering into its dust.

Alice Oswald

WOMAN IN A MUSTARD FIELD

From love to light my element
was altered when I fled
out of your house to meet the space
that blows about my head.

The sun was rude and sensible,
the rivers ran for hours
and whoops I found a mustard field
exploding into flowers;

and I slowly came to sense again
the thousand forms that move
all summer through a living world
that grows without your love.

My Neighbour, Mrs Kersey

That noise, Mrs Kersey—were you listening?
A tin roof warping and booming . . .

Our sitting rooms connect like shears
into the screw-pin of our fires.

We share a bird's nest in a common chimney.
If I'm right, you breathe, Mrs Kersey,

close as a dream-self on the other side.
This wall, if you just rubbed an eyelid,

is a bricked-up looking glass.
And wind across that roof's a loss

of difference to whatever's moving
privately through our heads this evening.

Like the clicking of my jaw,
the tic-tac of your solitaire.

Ian Pople

THE SAME CONDEMNATION

There were not too many of us, I always felt
and I was always so glad of that,
that there were never too many of us.
It did, for example, at the very least,
grant an uninterrupted view of the river.

A crane like a single spider's leg.
And I imagine a man climbing
to the cab of the crane would wonder,
when he returned to earth, where was the earth.
And I never had the feeling, if I may use

so prosaic an image, of being the torn half
of a bus ticket, as I would surely have done
had there been more of us, and less uncertainty.
I have always found in my dealings with you
that a certain uncertainty has led

to a feeling of closer acquaintanceship;
a rather British feeling, one suspects,
in this day and age. And one that,
I hasten to add, I could not have shared
with the others. Not that they were

insensitive men; they were, each in his own way,
the very milk of human kindness,
whatever one might have read to the contrary,
and later. But uncertainty was their stock-in-trade
as it were, whereas I am, and always

have been, a rather nervous man.
susceptible always to the firm handshake,
the misted car, to Norrie's moments
for lightening the atmosphere, as much as
I recognised how that irritated James.

Huddled, as in a rainy bus-shelter,
amidst these uncertain friends, you yearn,
like the landlord's dog, for comfort.
And when the comfort of events was set
in train, I imagined us a set of boys

catching the bus to town, on a Saturday morning,
ground cigarette ash, bus breath
already half a morning used (my father
'Some of us work on Saturdays, you know.')
and further up the cambered top deck of the bus,

a single woollen glove. As it was,
these pictures were not too far from the truth.
For when we left the pub, they in their car,
we in ours, I had, as I have had before,
and dare say will again, a feeling

of running above the common-mill of things
as if I too sang in the outermost branches.
And this was so even as we crossed,
and recrossed, the soft illogical river,
to wait beside a lorry in a lay-by, its engine running.

FELLOW TRAVELLERS

The train begins our slow drift back
down through the boney mountains
to the cultivation of the valley floor.

Perhaps she feels herself a widow already,
clutching narcissi to her half-open coat,
and staring through the window,

like Sharaku's actor staring at the priest.
Perhaps there is a map among the trees.
In the stillness of the bird's head

is the movement of the stem it holds.
I lent boots to her quiet husband
and we crossed the fields to visit

the baptistry window: three hares
that dance endlessly in a circle,
and iron nails twisted in a crucifix,

the naked, halting fire of the man beneath;
to handle the book as if it was his own,
as if the marks there were made by him.

The Best Individual Poems

Patricia Beer

ART HISTORY

I am the man in the pink hat
Who catches everybody's eye
And is not really there.

In the preparatory version
My hat was dowdy,
I was older.
Now I am 'Who is that good-looking man?'
My brim is wide and bumptious.

I am immune, though hemmed in
By people working miracles,
Waving their arms about
In paeans of caring.

I am better dressed
Than goody-two-sleeves, Francis Xavier.
My robe is off-white silk
And pours down me like warm rain.
His is black and catches on his bones.

I hate do-gooders.
I believe the Good Samaritan
Sprang from behind a sharp rock
And mugged the man who famously went down
From Jerusalem to Jericho.
At the right moment he returned
With oil and wine and succour
And lives for ever.

Francis Xavier is bound to get to heaven
And he will no doubt pray for me
If I and my pink dynasty of hats
Are spared like late roses.
I have no heart for others,
He has none for himself.

Look, the dead rise up as white as candles,
With flame-coloured hair.
There is no room nor breath for them,
The air is stuffed with angels.
I am not giving up my place,
I have none,
Though I am central to this resurrection.

David Constantine

BOMBSCARE

But we have bombscares. There was one this spring
The day before my birthday. I went in wanting
The OS map of another island
And sniffed the hush, the hush and a change in the air,
The two together: spring come and a bombscare.

A plastic tape was run all around the centre
Slight and symbolic as a sabbath wire
And nobody transgressed. The sentries
Had nothing much to do, but everyone expelled
From making a living in the centre idled

In shirt sleeves and blouses on the first day warm enough
With those kept out. You feel let off
Idling on the outside if you have to. Inside
It's like a site two thousand years from now
Uncovered clean. A police car like a UFO,

The blue light twirling. You feel absolved
More still when word comes out the thing was shelved
Among the goods a year ago at least.
The thought of it lying where you often came and went,
Its time not yet, is like a present

Coming from where you could not know one might. The tape
Ran to the shop but let me in. Sat on the step
In the sort of respite Sunday mornings used to make
Or overnight deep snow. Sat in the sun
And opened the map of another island there and then.

On the empty blue it floats like an elm-seed.
Seems mostly rock. The thin yellow road,
Run from a steamer route on the east coast,
Includes some tumuli, a standing stone or two,
A ruined oratory in the noose of its lasso.

Fifty tomorrow. From off the west coast
Peninsulars push out. The one pushing the farthest,
I fix on that. Sweet, sitting in the sun
While a man with nifty fingers whose job it is,
Breathing quietly, makes a timebomb harmless.

Maura Dooley

The Message

How, at an open window the wind
filled a shirt with the shape of his body,
pressed it flat as an idea again.

Then, turning back the covers one still night
she found a bat in her bed, cupped it,
flung its small warmth into the sky.

But, the need for a cigarette
was the need to press hard on the wheel
of his Zippo: pain, ignition.

So, when the parcel came she wasn't surprised
that all his curls spilled out
clipped, abundant and with no message.
Somewhere, his head was cool and clear and free.

Kathleen Jamie

The Graduates

If I chose children they'd know
stories of the old country, the place
we never left. I swear

I remember no ship
slipping from the dock,
no cluster of hurt, proud family,

waving till they were wee
as china milkmaids
on a mantelpiece,

but we have surely gone,
and must knock with brass
kilted pipers

doors to the old land;
we emigrants of no farewell
who keep our bit language

in jokes and quotes;
our working knowledge
of coal-pits, fevers: lost

like the silver bangle I lost
at the shows one Saturday
tried to conceal, denied

but they're not daft;
and my bright, monoglot bairns
will discover, misplaced

among the book-shelves,
proof, rolled in a red tube:
my degrees, a furled sail, my visa.

Les Murray

THE EARLY DARK

As the woman leaves the nursery, driving into early dark,
potholes in the lane make plants nudge and the wire-caged

fowls cluck like crockery, in the back of the station wagon.
A symphony is ending, too, over the brilliant city-plan

of the dashboard, and clapping pours like heavy rain
for minutes, outdoing the hoarse intake of asphalt

till her son giggles *I like that best, the applause part.*
He's getting older; now he has to win odd exchanges.

She's still partly back in the huge wind-wrangled sheet shed
with its pastels and parterres of seedlings, level by table

and the shy nurseryman, his eyes like a gatecrasher's fork
at a smorgasboard, spiking and circling. Now each object

in the headlights is unique, except the constant supplying
of trees, apparitional along verges, in near pastures. An owl

wrenches sideways off the road's hobnail; a refrigerator, shot
for children to breathe in it, guards someone's parcels; a boot.

A turn past this rollicking prewar bridge marks an end to tar.
Now for the hills, balancing on the tyres' running-shoes.

These road-ripples, Mum, they're sound-waves, did you know?
is also a surrender, to soothe. She recalls a suitor she told

about beauty's hardships, and her lovers, married and not,
whom he'd know. It felt kinder, confiding in an unattractive man.

The Other Poems

Fergus Allen

A Time for Blushing
For Joan

Plain-clothes inspectors are operating in this store,
In this station and these offices, on every floor.

Dog is reportedly eating dog at the street corners
And television crews focus on the griefs of mourners,

But the inspectors are using listening devices
To harken to the angels calling the starting prices.

Like lymph, they lead shadowy lives, keeping out of sight,
And, like phagocytes, they are always in the right.

Sometimes we may spot them in alcoves, transmitting orders
Or murmuring into miniature tape recorders.

From attics above the bankers' plaza and its fountains,
Encrypted reports go to antennae on the mountains.

They move amongst us unnoticed, in lovat and fawn,
Catching us when we order a drink or mow the lawn.

From lairs in mock orange and dogwood, spectacled eyes
Interpret my movements, read my lips and note my lies,

And remotely controlled bees employ their working hours
Dictating my sins into the corollas of flowers.

The poplars flap their tongues on the far side of the wall,
And the plain-clothes inspectorate overhears it all.

So it's silence for us, my love, it's silence in bed –
And what I was about to say had better not be said.

Moniza Alvi

An Unknown Girl

In the evening bazaar
studded with neon
an unknown girl
is hennaing my hand.
She squeezes a wet brown line
from a nozzle.
She is icing my hand,
which she steadies with hers
on her satin-peach knee.
In the evening bazaar
for a few rupees
an unknown girl
is hennaing my hand.
As a little air catches
my shadow-stitched kameez
a peacock spreads its lines
across my palm.
Colours leave the street
float up in balloons.
Dummies in shop-fronts
tilt and stare
with their Western perms.
Banners for Miss India 1993,
for curtain cloth
and sofa cloth
canopy me.
I have new brown veins.
In the evening bazaar
very deftly
an unknown girl
is hennaing my hand.
I am clinging
to these firm peacock lines

like people who cling
to the sides of a train.
Now the furious streets
are hushed.

I'll scrape off
the dry brown lines
before I sleep,
reveal soft as a snail trail
the amber bird beneath.
It will fade in a week.
When India appears and reappears
I'll lean across a country
with my hands outstretched
longing for the unknown girl
in the neon bazaar.

John Ash

In Khorkum

the wounded bird sang in the tree
and the kings were remembered
when the mother wept and the father went away
leaving the red slippers for his son
who had stopped speaking
and the martyrs were remembered and the ancestors
who rode into battle on purple horses
and the bird still sang in the summit of the poplar
as a salt breeze blew in from the lake
where the boats sailed toward the island of the almonds
and the pruning implements writhed
on the blue wall of the house
longing to escape into the orchards
then the trees whispered prophecies
as they have done in Alexander of Macedon's day
and ravens' eggs were painted with the colours of the fields
where the earth crumbled under the horses' hooves
and the father sat in mid-ocean sailing to America
and the prince rode into the heart of the rock
the Raven's Rock the Rock of Van
and said: 'I will not come out
until the world is less wicked
until wheat grains grow as big as rosebuds'
but the world stayed wicked and the rock stayed shut
yet clouds like winged heads still rose above the mountains
and the boats sailed by where now there are none
and the boy found a voice in the wood
he had whittled for his father who was gone
then the scent of apricots covered the fields
and clear water ran in channels beside the streets of Van
below the rock into which the prince had vanished
then the uncle's body was thrown against the door
and the grandmother stepped in the blood

and God was dead for her
but the plough still sang in the fields
and the sun danced like a dervish in the trees
and one year later the son was born
and soon the father departed leaving the red slippers
and boats sailed toward the island of the almonds
where the palace of king Gagik had vanished
and candles burned before the tombs of the ancestors
and the prince said: 'I will not come out
until the world is less wicked
until barley grains are as large as walnuts'
and the earth could not bear the weight of his horse
then a regiment of butchers descended on the villages
then the fire rained down from the rock
then the fire ran through the fields
then the fire erased the images of the martyrs
then the demon sat above the fire in an elegant suit
amusing himself with a French novel
and the people of Shadakh were killed
and the people of Berghri and the people of Harput
then the mother buried everything she possessed
in the garden in Aikezdan
and the son and the mother left the homeland
walking day after day over the hard ground
eating wild herbs and unripe fruit
passing by Masis crossing river Arax
and four years later the mother died
still longing for the home of her ancestors
and the son travelled on to Tiflis to Batum and Bolis
sailing to America to the father he did not love
and the scent of the apricots followed him
the taste of the salt and cries of birds above the rock
then in poverty and long weeks of rain
his mother's embroidered apron began to unfold
and wheat grains grew big as rosebuds
then the paintings burned and the dead mother spoke:
'My son what can I do? Colour and contour

Have gone from my face, the light has gone from my eyes,
Scorpions nest in my heart. Child you have wandered
enough.'

John Ashbery

The Problem of Anxiety

Fifty years have passed
since I started living in those dark towns
I was telling you about.
Well, not much has changed. I still can't figure out
how to get from the post office to the swings in the park.
Apple trees blossom in the cold, not from conviction,
and my hair is the color of dandelion fluff.

Suppose this poem were about you—would *you*
put in the things I've carefully left out:
descriptions of pain, and sex, and how shiftily
people behave toward each other? Naw, that's
all in some book it seems. For you
I've saved the descriptions of chicken sandwiches,
and the glass eye that stares at me in amazement
from the bronze mantel, and will never be appeased.

Eleanor Brown

THE LADS

The lads, the lads, away the lads;
we are the Boys, who make this Noise: hoo, ha; hoo-*ha*;
a-*way*, awayawayaway, a-way, away;
ere we go, ere we go, ere we go;
we are the Boys, who make this Noise:
hoo *ha*.

Away the lads. I love your poetry.
It strips the artform down to nakedness,
distilling it to spirituous drops
of utter purity.
I like the way you shout it all so loud,
revelling in the shamelessness
of its repetitiousness; the way it never stops
delighting
you. You've every right to be proud
of your few, brief, oral formulae –
any of which will do, for *Match of the Day*,
or Friday night, Lads' Night Out,
lagered up and fighting –
you are the lads. You've every right to shout.

Your poetry belligerently asserts
what nobody would trouble to deny:
that you are the lads; that there you go;
that yours will never be to reason why.
My unsingable songs cannot do more for me
than rid me of my epicene disgust,
after I've served you all ten pints and watched
you flushing up with random rage and lust.

You'll smack each other's heads tonight
and shag each other's birds;
you are the Boys, who make this Noise.
What need have you for words?

We will not argue, therefore, you and I.
Your poetry serves your purpose; mine serves mine.
You only tell me what I don't deny,
and I don't tell you anything. That's fine.

Away, the lads. Your deathless chants will be
heard in these bars and streets long after we
are dead (for lads are mortal too); your sons
will never feel the need for different ones.

Ron Butlin

ADVERTISEMENT FOR A SCOTTISH SERVANT

Would you like a very Scottish servant all your own
who'll do for, spiritually speaking, you alone?
A lad o' pairts: a prophet, historian and more,
a therapist/composer who understands the score?
Guaranteed – your past and future contrapuntally combined
into a pre-determined present so defined
you'll never need to think or feel again!

Your gardener for life, his motto: prune first then restrain
the slightest sign of growth. He'll cut you down to size
(for your own good) then train your roots to do
their darkest: dig deep, grasp, immobilise;
if needs be, split your soul in two.
He'll anticipate your every beck and call –
he *kent your faither*, after all!

As a Scottish-school economist he takes great pains
where pain was never due. No credit-giving Keynes,
he soon has Adam Smith's close-fistedness outclassed
insisting every childhood trauma last
your lifetime. All you'll need to know is what he'll tell you,
even when you're sleeping he'll compel you
treat his dreams as if they were your own.

Say 'Yes' – he's yours! Your very own: flesh, blood and bone
passed on as Scottish fathers pass him on
to Scottish sons (with references supplied
unto the seventh generation). A tendency to patricide
but nothing serious – just words – so never heed him.
This very Scottish servant –
who needs him?

Ciaran Carson

ALIBI

Remorselessly, in fields and forests, on street corners,
    on the eternal
Altar of the bed, murder is done. Was I there? I
    stared into the terminal

Of my own mirrored pupil, and saw my eye denying it,
    like one hand
Washing clean the other. Where was I then? Everybody
    wears the same Cain brand

Emblazoned on their foreheads. I saw the deed and what
    it led to. Heard the shriek
As well. And then my eyes were decommissioned by the knife.
    But I saw him last week,

And I know he is amongst us. And no, I can't tell his
    name. What name would you
Make up for murderers of their own childhood, who
    believe lies to be true?

The lovers enter the marrowbone of a madman and succumb
    slowly in their pit
Of lime. A croaking black unkindness of ravens has
    cloaked it

With a counterfeit of corpses. All our words were in vain.
    What flag are we supposed
To raise above the citadel? Where should we go? All
    the roads are closed.

O ubiquitous surveillant God, we are accomplices to
    all assassinations.
Gag me, choke me, strangle me, and tell me that there
    are no further destinations.

And finally, it must be left unsaid that those not born
    to this, our vampire family,
Sleep soundly in their beds: they have the final alibi.

Harry Clifton

REDUCTIO

"I could spend the rest of my life simply drawing a table and two chairs".
– Alberto Gi acometti.

What is big? What is extended in space?
Not this studio, surely, not this glass
On a wooden table, or the apple
Trapped forever in the intersecting planes
Of redemptive vision. Certainly not this face –
But the rue d'Alesia, outside in the rain,
The millions of strange people
Whirled like atoms through the hub of Montparnasse

As night comes down, and the lit conceptual cages,
Dome, Select, Rotonde, the stamping-grounds
Of seeing and being seen, the gilt cafés
And mirrored brothels of the rue de l'Echaudée
Where goddesses file naked on the stage,
Invite appraisal, and your mind's hot foundry
Casts them in bronze, remote as steles,
Cycladic or Sumerian, ancestral but still real.

What is big? What is extended in space?
Not the little tin soldiers, oh so small
In toyshop windows, though they say it all.
Not the yellow decals, not the pedestrian lights,
Stationary Man, or Walking Man, in the night's
Electric statuary. Not the living gaze
Forever fugitive, but only the skull;
The pleasure-seekers after hours, crashed out

On benches and late metros, heads agape
In a staring void. *"All the living are dead"*
It suddenly hits you. No, not Woman now, not Tree –
And where did it get you, that theft of bread
In childhood? Not Paris now, but infinities
Of disconnected people, faces, times,
Humanity dissolving into shapes
At the ends of avenues, at the ends of rhymes.

What is big, now? What is extended in space?
A single tungsten bulb, a Palace-at-Four,
Your lean-to shed. Inside it, memory swarms
With ancient heads, in the depths of revolving doors
Beheld, forgotten . . . From table to wooden chair
Saharas spread. A glass suspended in air –
You take a drink. To keep your fingers warm
You busy yourself, with the one loved face
Attempted endlessly, with the one loved form.

Robert Crawford

CHAPS

With his Bible, his Burns, his brose and his baps
Colonel John Buchan is one of the chaps,
With his mother, his mowser, his mauser, his maps,
Winston S. Churchill is one of the chaps.

Chaps chaps chaps chaps
Chaps chaps chaps chaps

Rebecca Mphalele is one of the chaps,
Ezekiel Ng is one of the chaps,
Queenie Macfadzean is one of the chaps,
Kayode Nimgaonkar is one of the chaps.

Chaps chaps chaps chaps
Chaps chaps chaps chaps

Oxfordy chaps, Cambridgey chaps,
Glasgowy chaps, Harrovian chaps,
Oxfordy chaps, Cambridgey chaps,
Oxfordy chaps, Cambridgey chaps.

Chaps chaps chaps chaps
Chaps chaps chaps chaps

The sergeant's a chap, the rifle's a chap,
The veldt is a chap, the heather's a chap,
A great JCR of them tossing their caps
Like schoolboys at Eton dyed red on the maps.

Chaps chaps chaps chaps
Chaps chaps chaps chaps

The porthole's a chap, the cannon's a chap,
The Haigs and the Slessors, the Parks are all chaps,
Mungos and Maries, filling the gaps
In the Empire's red line that can never collapse.

Chaps chaps chaps chaps
Chaps chaps chaps chaps

Lord Kitchener needs them to pose for his snaps
Of Ypres and Verdun with chaps' heads in their laps
Singing Gilbert and Sullivan or outlining traps
To catch rowdies at Eights Week, next year perhaps.

Chaps chaps chaps chaps
Chaps chaps chaps chaps

The war memorial's a chap, the codebook's a chap,
The wind is a chap, the horse is a chap
The knitters, the padres, the limbs are all chaps
From Hawick and Africa, poppies are chaps

Chaps chaps chaps chaps
Chaps chaps chaps chaps

Kevin Crossley-Holland

THE LANGUAGE OF YES

This world's wreckers are at their games
and everywhere it is late.

Words words words a fury of words
hype and shred and prate,
sanitise, speculate;
they please themselves.

How can I be content
with hollow professions
or the arm's length of the sceptic?
Even with the sensory,
the pig heart's slop-and-mess?

I still want.

Let me make and remake the word
which reveals itself,
unexpected, always various,

and be so curious
(affirmation's mainspring)
I sing the language of yes.

Allen Curnow

PACIFIC 1945-1995
A Pantoum

>   if th'assassination
> could trammel up the consequence, and catch,
> with his surcease, success; that but this blow
> might be the be-all and the end-all . . . here,
> but here, upon this bank and shoal of time
> we'ld jump the life to come
> Macbeth

Quantifiable griefs. The daily kill.
  One bullet, with his name on, his surcease.
'The casualties were few, the damage nil' –
  The scale was blown up, early in the piece.

One bullet, with his name on, his surcease.
  Laconic fire, short work the long war mocks.
The scale was blown up, early in the piece –
  How many is few? After the aftershocks,

laconic fire – short work! The long war mocks,
  dragging out our dead. What calibration says
how many is few, after the aftershocks
  of just such magnitude? We heard the news,

dragging out our dead. What calibration says,
  right! You can stop crying now, was it really
of just such magnitude? We heard the news
  again, the statistical obscene, the cheery

right! You can stop crying now, was it really
  the sky that fell, that boiling blue lagoon?
Again, the statistical obscene, the cheery
  salutation and bright signature tune.

The sky that fell! That boiling blue lagoon!
  Jacques Chirac's rutting tribe – with gallic
salutation and bright signature tune –
  thermonuclear hard-on. Ithyphallic

Jacques! Chirac's rutting tribe, with gallic
  eye for the penetrable, palm-fringed hole –
thermonuclear hard-on, ithyphallic
  BANG! full kiloton five below the atoll.

Eye for the penetrable, palm-fringed hole,
  whose trigger-finger, where he sat or knelt down –
BANG! full kiloton five, below the atoll
  had it off, bedrock deep orgasmic meltdown –

whose trigger-finger, where he sat or knelt down,
  fifty years back, fired one as huge as then
had it off bedrock deep, orgasmic meltdown –
  whose but Ferebee's? – Hiroshima come again! –

fifty years back, fired one as huge as then
  fireballed whole cities while 'People . . . copulate, pray . . .'
Whose but Ferebee's – Hiroshima come again –
  bombardier, US Army? *Enola Gay*

fireballed whole cities while 'People . . . copulate, pray . . .'
  Not God fingering Gomorrah but the man,
bombardier, US Army. *Enola Gay*
  shuddering at 30,000 feet began –

not God fingering Gomorrah, but the man,
  the colonel her pilot who named her for his Mom –
shuddering at 30,000 feet began –
  'Little Boy' delivered – her run for home:

the colonel her pilot, who named her for his Mom,
  flew her to roost (at last) in the Smithsonian.

'Little Boy' delivered, her run for home
    lighter for the Beast's birth, her son's companion:

flew her to roost (at last) in the Smithsonian:
    are tourists' hearts and hopes, viewing her there,
lighter for the Beast's birth, her son's companion?
    Jacques' Marianne's confinement, is that near?

Are tourists' hearts and hopes, viewing her there,
    pronounced infection-free and safely tested –
Jacques' Marianne's confinement, is that near? –
    What effluent, what fall-out can be trusted?

pronounced infection-free and safely tested
    for carcinogenic isotope unseen fall-out –
what effluent, what fall-out can be trusted?
    The Beast once born, who's answering the call-out?

For carcinogenic isotope, unseen fall-out,
    for the screaming city under the crossed hairs,
the Beast once born. Who's answering the call-out,
    no time even to know it's one of THEIRS –

for the screaming city under the crossed hairs,
    'The casualties were few, the damage nil' –
No time even to know! It's one of theirs –
    quantifiable griefs. The daily kill.

Alan Dixon

A Fearsome Sister

Indignant sister, strong and square
As pigsty gate, with nunty hair,
Has nothing else (she lies) to wear
But things from charities that scare
     And fight together.

Her equatorial dry speech
– The perfect vehicle to teach
A brother not to overreach –
Makes her more prickly pear than peach.
     She'll swing her leather

And truss me in an old spud sack
And rope her piano on my back,
Whip me to Iboland and whack
Along a tangled Spanish track
     In beach-bum weather.

'Where are those candlesticks?' she'll yap
Each time she cuts me with her strap.
She'll only let me kneel and lap
Mud when she's thumping her Scotch snap
     For mad dead mother.

Theo Dorgan

THE MATCH DOWN THE PARK
for Na Piarsaigh on their fiftieth anniversary

Tom Knott comes bulling out, his shoulder down
bringing weight to bear on the sliothar dropping
From his hand. The crack of ash on leather echoes
The length of the Park.

Like a new evening star, the ball
Climbs the November air, a clean
White flash in the cold and cloud.

All of the faces around me turn
Like plates to the sky, tracking the rising arc.
Over the halfway line now, and dropping into
A clash of hurleys, forward shouldering back.

Our jerseys are brighter than theirs
In this eerie light, the black and amber
Fanning out into a line, a berserk charge.

My face is jammed through the flat bars
Of the gate, the goalposts make me dizzy
Leaning back to look up. Their goalie is jittery,
The chocolate melts in my fist, I hear myself

Howling from a great distance
Come on Piarsaigh, come on, face up, face up . . .
Sound stops in a smell of mud and oranges,

I can feel the weight of them bearing down on goal,
I can't see, Mr. Connery is roaring, and
Johnny Parker,
I bet even my Dad is roaring, back there in the crowd
But I can't leave the gate to go see, I can't –

A high ball, a real high one, oh God
Higher than the moon over the fence towards Blackrock,
It's dropping in, they're up for it, Pat Kelleher's fist

Closes on leather, knuckles suddenly badged with blood
In the overhead clash, he steadies, digs in his heel,
He turns, shoots from the 21 –
The whole field explodes in my face

A goal! A goal! Their keeper stretched across his line,
His mouth filled with mud, the sliothar feet from my face,
A white bullet bulging the net.

Everything stops.

A ship comes gliding on the high tide, her hull
Floating through the elms over the rust-red stand.
A man on the flying-bridge looks down on us.

I race back to my father, threading the crowd,
Watching for heavy boots, neck twisting back
To the net still bulging, the ship still coming on,
The green flag stabbed aloft, the final whistle.

Sixpence today for the bikeminder under his elm.
Men in dark overcoats greeting my Dad
Well done Bert, ye deserved it. And
A great game, haw? Ah dear God what a goal!

I'm introduced as the eldest fella. *Great man yourself.*
Men anxious to be home, plucking at bikes, pushing away.
The slope to the river, the freighter drawing upstream.

And then the long, slow pedal home,
Weaving between the cars on Centre Park Road,
Leaning back into the cradle of his arms.

That was some goal, wasn't it Dad?
It was indeed, it was. His breath warm on my neck,
A wave for the man on Dunlop's gate,
We'll pass the ship tied up near City Hall.

He's a knacky hurler, Pat Kelleher.
    He is Dad, ah jay he is.
By God, that was the way to win.
    It was, Dad, it was.

Mark Doty

NEW DOG

Jimi and Tony
can't keep Dino,
their cocker spaniel;
Tony's too sick,
the daily walks
more pressure
than pleasure,
one more obligation
that can't be met.

And though we already
have a dog, Wally
wants to adopt,
wants something small
and golden to sleep
next to him and
lick his face.
He's paralyzed now
from the waist down,

whatever's ruining him
moving upward, and
we don't know
how much longer
he'll be able to pet
a dog. How many men
want another attachment,
just as they're
leaving the world?

Wally sits up nights
and says, *I'd like
some lizards, a talking bird,
some fish. A little rat.*

So after I drive
to Jimi and Tony's
in the Village and they
meet me at the door and say,
We can't go through with it,

we can't give up our dog,
I drive to the shelter
– just to look – and there
is Beau: bounding and
practically boundless,
one brass concatenation
of tongue and tail,
unmediated energy,
too big, wild,

perfect. He not only
licks Wally's face
but bathes every
irreplaceable inch
of his head, and though
Wally can no longer
feed himself he can lift
his hand, and bring it
to rest on the rough gilt

flanks when they are,
for a moment, still.
I have never seen a touch
so deliberate.
It isn't about grasping;
the hand itself seems
almost blurred now,
softened, though
tentative only
because so much will
must be summoned,
such attention brought
to the work – which is all
he is now, this gesture
toward the restless splendor,
the unruly, the golden,
the animal, the new.

Lauris Edmond

THE PACE OF CHANGE

'Not unconscious, no. The patient's
brain died hours ago.' But look – your skin
is warm to touch; lying back, eyes closed,
you labour fiercely. Something in you
cries out still for struggle, effort:
this is how it is to be alive, to fight
moment by moment to achieve each
rasping, shuddering sob of breath.

I lean down, labouring too, as if by
endlessly repeating names of things
we know I can reverse the tide of blood
they say has taken you. Nothing changes.
Stupidly I try again. Then see at last
the body's terrible sorrow. Poor breath,
that cannot speak a word: how shrewd,
how manifold were once its languages.

Steve Ellis

GARDENERS' QUESTION TIME

Well, after lagging your tubers
nest them deep in the airing-cupboard.
If you cadge your wife's old vest
it snugs 'em down lovely,
you'll get interest on your warmth in May.

Shallots, the wardrobe: my great-uncle
would entertain no other store.
In the darkness, festoon them on hangers,
you'll have to evict the wife's hats
but you'll be munching on plumpness in May.

A pair of knickers strains barrel-water
best, and I'll say something else:
if you can borrow your wife's bra
it's a smashing cradle to ripen peaches,
trembling on the washing-line in June,

scarcely reining their softness, for you.
As for mulch, there's nothing matches
blood & bone. If she's dead lately,
put your wife through the shredder,
(ask her first) and scatter it thick.

You'll be in that deckchair in August,
lungs full of lush green peace,
just you, your life, and the shed. Heaven.

Adèle Geras

THE SUITOR

Mother, on first acquaintance
he is not to my taste.

(Put him in the Yellow Room.
Gather me into my garments.)

His coat glitters like cockroaches.
His boots contain nightmares.

(Pull the flat maids out
from between grey sheets.)

His fingernails are white;
unreasonably curved.

(At eleven o'clock the family portraits
open their mouths to scream.)

Wallpaper absorbs and disperses
the shadow of his hat.

(I am wearing a bustle.
I am wearing a corset.
I am wearing a hat
with a veil; with a black veil.)

Tears leave stains
at the bottom of teacups.
Sighs become cobwebs.

Mother, have you seen them?
Mother, is it rude to speak of them?
There, there, thrusting between his shoulderblades
he has a pair of ribbed and leathery wings.

(He will spread them.
They will mask the light;
groan and flap like an umbrella
in an ecstasy of wind.
They will fall into dry folds
when he is done with them.)

Put him in the Yellow Room.
Let me consider.

David Hart

This is the vessel. The bodies, as you can see,
have rotted further since I sent you the note,

and couch grass has begun to grow through the deck.
Where there was a log book there is now pulp.

I have done my best with devotion hoping you'd come;
I was a bright lad at school, though inward and shy.

Before you make your inspection of the remains
inch by inch perhaps you would like lunch: aperatif

squeezed fresh from wild raspberries, then nettle soup,
main course of Rock Salmon, a slippery

Orange Squash I've been keeping cool in the river,
goosegog dumplings to follow, then a tea bag

preserved these years in dock leaves. I crave
company but without your permission

I shall inflict on you no conversation,
and after a short sleep you can soldier on

through what's left of daylight into the night.
It is entirely up to you, I am your servant.

John Hughes

1812

When I tried to hold onto the wind
with my rotten teeth
my horse took fright and bolted.

As soon as I lost sight of it
two corporals of Napoleon's Grand Army
slaughtered it for lunch and dinner.

After he'd studied the fly-blown carcass,
downwind and from twenty metres off,
the local savant calculated
the soldiers had eaten
seven per cent of the animal.

Why does it give me pleasure to say
it was snowing the day
I set out for Moscow
to lay the horse's skull
at the emperor's swollen feet?

August Kleinzahler

SNOW IN NORTH JERSEY

Snow is falling along the Boulevard
and its little cemeteries hugged by transmission shops
and on the stone bear in the park
and the WWI monument, making a crust
on the soldier with his chinstrap and bayonet
It's blowing in from the west
over the low hills and meadowlands
swirling past the giant cracking stills
that flare all night along the Turnpike
It is with a terrible deliberateness
that Mr Ruiz reaches into his back pocket
and counts out $18 and change for his Lotto picks
while in the upstairs of a thousand duplexes
with the TV on, cancers tick tick tick
and the snow continues to fall and blanket
these crowded rows of frame and brick
with their heartbreaking porches and castellations
and the red '68 Impala on blocks
and Joe he's drinking again and Myra's boy Tommy
in the old days it would have been a disgrace
and Father Keenan's not been having a good winter
and it was nice enough this morning
till noon anyhow with the sun sitting up there like a crown
over a great big dome of mackerel sky
But it's coming down now, all right
falling on the Dixon-Crucible Pencil factory
and on the spur to Bayonne
along the length of the Pulaski Skyway
and on St Bridgit's and the Alibi Saloon
closed now, oh dear, I can't remember how long
and lordjesussaveus they're still making babies
and what did you expect from this life
and they're calling for snow tonight and through tomorrow

an inch an hour over 9 Ridge Road and the old courthouse
and along the sluggish, gray Passaic
as it empties itself into Newark Bay
and on Grandpa's store that sells curries now
and St Peter's almost made it to the semis this year
It's snowing on the canal and railyards, the bus barns and trucks
and on all the swells in their big houses along the river bluff
It's snowing on us all
and on a three-storey fix-up off of Van Vorst Park
a young lawyer couple from Manhattan bought
where for no special reason in back of a closet
a thick, dusty volume from the Thirties sits open
with a broken spine and smelling of mildew
to a chapter titled *Social Realism*

Michael Laskey

THE VISITATION

It was Kay sleeping that woke me.
For once she was breathing so deeply,
so slowly, I had to break surface.

From the landing I heard a movement
downstairs, in the sitting-room surely,
like a cartilage clicking, the rocking-

chair maybe, but nothing alarming
or furtive, so I stood in the open
doorway and switched on the light.

'I took out the bulb' said a voice
that had to be Nick's. 'There's a moth
I've been taking some photos of here

and I don't want it burnt. Come and see.'
Through the darkness he reached an arm
round my shoulder and pointed the beam

of his torch at the curtain in the bay
where a small moth clung, its green wings
intricately speckled and veined

white and black. There was no need to speak
about Lesley or why he'd left them.
Or why I'd written just once.

'It's a Merveille du Jour,' he told me.
'Not at all rare.'

Marion Lomax

DIVIDED WE STAND

You are looking at me now like the man from Special Branch
who scrutinised my face when I waited to board the plane.
I thought – somewhere there must be a terrorist with my eyes –
I expected to be stopped. He waved everyone straight through.

I came separate, out of place, through my own act of faith.
You stood among families waiting to be completed –
but I had never promised. Doubts soon sabotaged your smile.
Now we move from room to room switching on and off the lamps.

I wake before dawn. A bang: my bed is scattered with glass –
shards, glimmers, jagged pieces. The floor is sharp, clothes covered.
You fill the doorway, lift me; my feet touch down in your room –
'Keep right back from the window!' – but outside the street is calm.

An empty chair, a towel – your clothes are tidied away.
Only the bed is betrayed, the imprint of your body.
You do not declare your fear, your craving. No crucifix
clings to the wall, yet your eyes are praying into the dark.

At the side of the curtain we peer down to a pavement
which keeps its feet a secret under a stone-blinded lamp.
You are looking at me now as if you hope I'll declare
a shared religion or guilt, something that might help us cry.

The closed door has a halo. Shut out, shut in, it's the same.
You hold me pressed against you; pick the glass out of my hair.

E A Markham

STAND-IN

They spent decades tracking the children:
not much to go by, no names, a hint only of the parents
when young. They lost heart when the serial novel
of refugees threw up a happy episode on the news. Each relived
the other's life, visiting old haunts, pondering
partners that might have been. The fun of it –
as with all addiction – was knowing you could give it up
if you tried. And then one day they gave it up.

And they would celebrate the things not gone missing
in their lives, and not resent the sight of twosomes *everywhere*
settling for second best, in time doing better
than they feared (ha!) – their narratives more readable now.
So it's not the same when he fumbles the stand-in
and she remembers him as someone else.

Adrian Mitchell

Moving Poem

I'll call my new house 'REALITY'
Or maybe 'BOURGEOIS STATE'.
Its name will be burned on a slice of wood
And screwed to my garden gate.
When they say 'Hey, sticking a name on your house
Is a very suburban trait!'
I'll look up from the corpse I am eating
And say: 'This is the suburbs, mate.'

Paul Muldoon

THE HUG

(in memory of Joseph Brodsky)

'Of course, of course, of course,' I heard you intone
in your great peaches-and-diesel tenor
as I drew up to the airport in Cologne,
'there's an Auden in every Adenauer

though politicians and poets embrace, you see,
only before a masque or after a massacre.'
We sat with our daughters on our knees.
Poets and politicians are close . . . Close but no Cigar.'

You would break the filter-tip off a Camel –
'They're infinitely better "circumcised"' –
and pour another Absolut, *du lieber Himmel,*
eschewing absolutely the lemon-zest.

You had such gusto, Joseph: for an afternoon trip
to the hallowed ground of Middagh Street;
dim sum in Soho, all those bits and bobs of tripe
and chickens' gizzards and chickens' feet

and dumplings filled with gristle
that reminded you of a labor-camp
near Archangel. As I left the church of Saint Ursula
yesterday afternoon, I was already quite overcome

by the walls of *die Goldene Kammer*
swagged with human bones, already quite taken aback
by its abecedary, its Latin grammar,
of fibulas and femurs, its rack

of shanks and shoulderblades,
when a blast of air from, I guess, the Caucasus
threw its arms around me in the Ursulaplatz
with what was surely your 'Kisses, kisses, kisses.'

Sharon Olds

Mrs Krikorian

She saved me. When I arrived in sixth grade
a known criminal, the new teacher
asked me to stay after school the first day, she said
I've heard about you. She was a tall woman,
with a deep crevice between her breasts,
and a large, calm nose. She said,
This is a special library pass.
As soon as you finish your hour's work –
that hour's work that took ten minutes
and then the devil glanced into the room
and found me empty, a house standing open –
you can go to the library. Every hour
I'd zip through the work, and slip out of
my seat as if out of God's side and sail
down to the library, down through the empty
powerful halls, flash my pass
and stroll over to the dictionary
to look up the most interesting word
I knew, *spank,* dipping two fingers
into the jar of library paste to
suck that tart mucilage as I
came to the page with the cocker spaniel's
silks curling up like the fine steam of the body.
After *spank,* and *breast,* I'd move on
to *Abe Lincoln* and *Helen Keller,*
safe in their goodness till the bell, thanks
to Mrs Krikorian, amiable giantess
with the kind eyes. When she asked me to write
a play, and direct it, and it was a flop,
and I hid in the coat closet, she bought me a candy-cane
as you lay a peppermint on the tongue, and the worm
will come up out of the bowel to get it.
And so I was emptied of Lucifer

and filled with school glue and eros and
Amelia Earhart, saved by Mrs Krikorian.
And who had saved Mrs Krikorian?
When the Turks came across Armenia,
who slid her into the belly of a quilt, who
locked her in a chest, who mailed her to America?
And *that* one, who saved *her*, and *that* one –
who saved *her*, to save the one
who saved Mrs Krikorian, who was
standing there on the sill of sixth grade, a
wide-hipped angel, smoky hair
standing up lightly all around her head?
I end up owing my soul to so many,
to the Armenian nation, one more soul someone
jammed behind a stove, drove
deep into a crack in a wall,
shoved under a bed. I would wake
up, in the morning, under my bed – not
knowing how I had got there – and lie
in the dusk, the dustballs beside my face
round and ashen, shining slightly
with the eerie comfort of what is neither good nor evil.

Ruth Padel

A Drink in the New Piazza
In Memoriam Gerry Macnamara

I
They were switching on headlights
through A40 dusk, despite
the blaze from Mister Lighting

and a glow-worm trek of aeroplane
through the scuffed cloud:
a written line, a last letter

running left to right
of the flyover
till it smudged out in coughs.

The little source drawing south,
away from its end: that soft
broken run of cotton commas.

II
Driving west,
I took your sea-grass stairs
with me. As if,

if I kept them accurate
you wouldn't go. Perivale.
Wycombe. 'Nearly New Cars'.

On all of them I laid
roan tiles from your kitchen
with its open garden door,

a house with a white inside
and a green-gray empty shirt
on the floor

of a bathroom tessellated blue,
a master-design in Ming
for you – who knew the entire score

of *The Sound of Music*
and didn't want to be cremated
because it just might hurt.

Who'd asked me to your funeral
before you died.
To sing.

III
By some miracle you pulled
my breath, choked in London flu
as well as tears, did soar

up the ribs of St Xavier, more
or less as it was meant to do,
beyond where you were lying,

not on the sofa of
your late-night den
with its driftwood press

and Allegro, Allegro, Largo,
in a box that had not a thing
to do with you.

IV
The earth bit was worst
and you'd thought of that too
when you vetoed Dido's *Lament*

('Too sad'). The thud of lilies
that could only be the thud
of lilies, nothing else –

or the first shot of *Dr Zhivago*.
The mound of pinkish clay
against those tungsten hills,

and two hefty men
walking away from it,
back to HQ

after a good half-day
swinging from post-sacramental torsos
the straps that lowered you.

V
But Gerry, the way you held
everyone, all two
or three hundred, close all day!

The way you went
on All Saints Eve, telling everyone
through the mobile phone

it was all right, you were OK,
it was like a new city, something of Rome
but narrower. You could half-see

the mazy streets. As if you'd registered
at twilight
and were on the brink

of going out,
checking your jeans carefully
for change – ducat, piastre,

rouble – and passport,
Visacard, your hotel key:
for a drink in the new piazza.

M R Peacocke

GOOSE HYMN

We lub us ogre
It like we   two legi
Two blue eye
It dict us born

It warm us   dict us lib
It look us lub   feed us
goin out   comin in
Mind it mangly boot

It go unwingly
Lub it corni corni cop ya
Mind it strangly finger
it strongly anger

It frighten we
It mighty mighty alway
It might alway
might dict us die

Mario Petrucci

FOETAL DREAM

Wrinkled ginger-bread boy
sixteen millimetres long

with a half-life of half-an-hour
without the womb's dank oxygen.

The lad cycles it over, pocket-
wrapped in a muff of wool.

Just like that. She signs
the docket, then retreats: pulls

off her skirt to insert – almost
forgets to add the water first.

Like aquarium-feed, the enzymic
batter flakes away – reveals

fish-bud perfection: the headlet
of knobbled sard, bloodless

pearl-pricks of knuckles. A fist
already clenched, growing, hard.

Top Our Road, Bottom Our Road

Dat de way it alway been, say Mum:
de top and de bottom. And we at de bottom.
Suny day, I see house at top our road –
big roof, big window-no-wood-in, big car.
But we OK – got three room for we six,
plenny carboard to burn, patch up window-smash.
Pub at top our road got panellin
and carvery and car park. Our pub
all smoke and sausage and fisticuff.
Top de road got anteak shop,
wedding-cake shop, state agent. We got
crooky grocer, coal shop, porn broker.

One day, ask Mum if I can get to top our road.
She say: yes, mebbe – if you strong nuff, if you
ruthless nuff, lucky nuff. But it bluddy hard
climb. I suprise she swear. I surprise
she keep talk about roof. Roof alway leak anyway.
Anyway, she don't know, but I thinking:
come one day not too soon, world
give it last revolution. Den our road flip arse
over elbow, send all dat high people tumble
down. Den see who at top.
Dis belief.

Peter Porter

A SECRET LIFE

Lucky the self-exposers whose bad actions
Are sexual and may be confided to a diary
To illustrate the power of class and money
Or made the pillow-books of hot imagining.

Such pose a base where energy's forgiven,
Where anything is better than not doing,
And Blake's the brothel-keeper, and St. Paul's blunt
God Forbid! is snubbed by Grace Abounding.

But quite another life is here on offer,
A discontent rehearsing doubt like angles
Found before a mirror, the hoarding of endearments
Not believed in in a world devoid of value.

Cornered by angel, devil or sub-poena'd
By some long-anticipated court, this private
Bluebeard pleads a favourite legend – he's had
To lock them up, wife, mother, women, anyone.

His certain death's the fabled true belovèd
He hopes he'll never find. Could anything be
More convincing to a body than just ageing?
Will twenty-four hours fill with words and music?

The public life goes on. It has its trials:
They must be faced, and after the outfacing
Return in strength in dreams. This morning, Depression;
Tonight, a fierce headmaster prowling classrooms.

Yet no philosophy supports this. Which is
Why he carpenters his own provincial dogma
And makes a desperate wish: that he's not dreaming
The only dream commensurate with fairness.

His brain is walled with magic fictions, numbing
Itself with sex at last, crude Cockaigning
Far from desert vigils, as if his judges,
Knowing death's bad faith, might rule in pity
His secret life should paraphrase his dying.

Tom Pow

Leona

Leona, the wisdom of the village,
sits on her haunches on the new-swept earth
before a heap of plantain. Fried they will make
that night's only meal. She skims a large knife
under the green peel, then cuts the white flesh
in half and drops it in a cracked, blue basin.
Now and again she stops to brush her brow
with the back of her hand: elegant, assured.
Her husband is out of work. *Trabajo?*
There's none around here. I hear him playing
with a toddler-child inside their wooden
kitchen-shack. And hear the overloud clacks
of the domino players, chap-chapping
in the strained light beneath the lemon tree.
The same ones yesterday, today, tomorrow.

Over in the tiny village store, rich
with the clammy smells of coconut and rum,
a sixteen year old mother turns her chair
from the orange glow of the kerosene lamp
to suckle her baby in the half dark.
Half interested, a young brother looks on.
Añiano serves everyone in rota,
one item at a time. Unschooled, he scrubs
his calculator of its thin web
of numbers and tries again. At the last
he turns its bland face to the customer
in apology for what *it* has done.

Leona has determined her eldest
of four will not get pregnant at sixteen.
No *novios* for Juliana yet.
At seven each morning she must put on
a plain, blue blouse and take the truck to school
with the other girls. But each afternoon
she has English lessons down on the beach,
choosing the scantiest of chic dresses
from a glossy, coloured catalogue.

Craig Raine

HEAVEN ON EARTH

Now that it is night,
you fetch in the washing
from outer space,

from the frozen garden
filmed like a kidney,
with a ghost in your mouth,

and everything you hold,
two floating shirts, a sheet,
ignores the law of gravity.

Only this morning,
the wren at her millinery,
making a baby's soft bonnet,

as we stopped by the spring,
watching the water
well up in the grass,

as if the world were teething.
It was heaven on earth
and it was only the morning.

Christopher Reid

Two Dogs on a Pub Roof

There are two dogs on a pub roof.
One's called Garth, the other Rolf.
Both are loud – but don't think they're all mouth.
I've been watching them and it's my belief
that they've been posted there, not quite on earth,
as emissaries of some higher truth
it's our job to get to the bottom of,
if only we can sort out the pith from the guff.
Garth's bark's no ordinary *woof, woof*:
it's a full-throttle affair, like whooping-cough,
a racking hack that shakes him from scruff
to tail in hour-long binges of holding forth
on all manner of obsessive stuff,
from pigeons and planes to not getting enough
to eat and so being ready to bite your head off.
He's whipped up in a perpetual froth
of indignation on his own behalf.
Poof! Dwarf! Oaf! Filth!
These and suchlike are among his chief
forms of salutation – and he means you, guv!
His whole philosophy, his pennyworth,
is 'All's enemy that's not self'
(with the provisional exception of his brother Rolf).
It's no joke and you don't feel inclined to laugh.
Rolf's even more frightening: his *arf! arf!*
seems designed to tear the sky in half,
every utterance an ultimate expletive,
every one a barbed shaft
aimed accurately at your midriff
and transfixing you with impotent wrath.
You and him. It bothers you both.
The thing's reciprocal, a north-south
axis that skewers the two of you like love.

You're David and Goliath, Peter and the Wolf,
Robin Hood and his Sheriff, Mutt and Jeff –
any ding-donging duo from history or myth
that's come to stand as a hieroglyph
for eternal foedom, non-stop strife,
the old Manichean fisticuffs
without which there'd be no story, no life,
and the whole cycle of birth, breath,
scoff, boff, graft, grief and death
would amount to so much waste of puff.
You're spiritual partners, hand in glove,
you and Rolfie, you and Garth,
you and the two of them up on that roof,
barking and hopping, acting tough,
flinging their taunts across the gulf
of the entire neighbourhood: *You lot down beneath!*
You got a diabolical nerve!
Who gave you permissson to breathe?
This is our gaff! This is our turf!
Don't even think of crossing our path,
if you happen to value what remains of your health!
One false move and we'll show you teeth . . .
And so on. Of course, that's only a rough
translation, but it will more or less serve,
being at least the gist of the riff
that bores you mad and drives you stiff
all day long. Night, too. Nights, they work shifts.
One sleeps, while the other faces the brave
task of keeping the moon at a safe
distance and making sure the stars behave.
Which is why there are two of them. If
you've begun to wonder. As you no doubt have.
Then sometimes they'll mount an all-night rave,
Garth dancing with Rolf, Rolf with Garth –
though there's nothing queer about these two psychopaths –
and you're the inevitable wallflower, on the shelf,
surplus to requirements. Only you can't stay aloof.

Like it or lump it, you're stuck in their groove.
The joint's jumping in every joist and lath
and nobody, but nobody, is going to leave.
You're as free an agent as the flame-fazed moth
that's in thrall, flamboyantly befuddled, and not fireproof.
You're party to the party, however loth.
You belong along. You're kin. You're kith.
You're living testimony to the preposition 'with'.
You're baby, bathwater and bath.
So don't dash out with your Kalishnikov
and hope to cut a definitive swathe
through the opposition. Don't throw that Molotov
cocktail. Put down that Swiss Army knife.
Stop spitting. Stop sputtering. Don't fluster. Don't faff.
And don't be so daft, naff, duff or uncouth
as to think you're calling anyone's bluff –
let alone that of the powers above –
by threatening to depart in a huff.
They are your world, where you live,
and this is what their telegraph
of yaps and yelps, their salvoes of snuff-
sneezes, their one-note arias, oath-
fests and dog-demagoguery, their throes of gruff
throat-flexing and guffaws without mirth
are meant to signify. And it's all for your behoof!
So thanks be to Garth, and thanks to Rolf –
those two soothsayers with their one sooth,
pontificating on that pub roof –
and thanks to the God who created them both
for your enlightenment and as proof of His ruth!

Mark Roper

RED HANDED

In the darkness of the church
I felt more than saw. Troubled
shadow, air scratching itself:
a small bird, locked in.

I opened the main door wide.
A bale of warm air fell in,
a cartoon invitation, spiced
with seed and faint sound.

The bird wouldn't buy it.
Over it flew and over against
the sealed chancel windows.
I'd never catch it and yet,

out of its element, estranged,
it seemed somehow we had met.
At length it lay down on
a limestone sill, staring up

at me, resigned. Entreaty
nerved the air between us.
I would carry it down, let it
go into the bright afternoon.

It wouldn't let me touch.
Always at the last moment flew.
There are no safe hands, all
have tasted money, or blood.

Carol Rumens

Best China Sky

A primrose crane, a slope of ochre stacks,
Stencilled on tissue-thin
Blue, and, flung between
These worlds, a sword-flash rainbow,
The cloud it lies against,
Metallic as its topmost skin,
And, round the eyes of hills,
Tha tender bluish-green
That quickly yellows.

The prism comes and goes:
Wonderful stain, transparency of art!
A smoke-wraith sails right through it.
But now it strengthens, glows and braves its span,
You'd think it was the rim
Of some resplendent turquoise plate,
Offering hills and cranes and streets and us
Fancies designed to melt
As our fingers touched them.

Lawrence Sail

Another Parting

Remember how we gunned the car down the motorway
Towards the airport's absurdly slow
Litanies of departure? – Check-in, the catechism
Of security questions, the electric angelus
Of chimes, passport control, the gate…

When, somehow, we managed to say
Goodbye, we felt we were being crushed
By the weight of time that had massed above us
Like the grey cloud into which you would go:
And, through it all, an orphan half-phrase
Rang in my head – but a mad contradiction
Of what was real – *Time that is given…*
Today, as another parting comes closer,
The words recur, along with that cloud
Which moves over each lived minute of love.

But today those minutes have all the brightness
Of your favourite gemstones – the steady burn
Of garnets, the amethyst's clear purple,
The mallow-green of malachite, with its swirl
Of black contours beneath the surface:
As if parting itself could just be
Like seeing sunlight pinch the ocean
Into points of sparkle, or like the way
In which now that phrase finds its sudden completion –
Time that is given has no shadow.

No shadow – simply the winking grains
Of all those minutes which fire and flare
Along the runways that lead into darkness:
And, beyond, the calm patterns of the stars,
The bearings which fix our new arrivals.

Penelope Shuttle

EIGHT FROG DREAMS

One
'A more innocent creature than the tree-frog
does not exist,' says Rennie–

'it is besides so little
and of so beautiful a green
that it is a very common pet in Germany.'

'In the autumn of 1830,' Rennie continues–
'I caught one sitting on a bramble at Cape La Hève . . .
which I kept for many weeks:

but it finally escaped from me
between Bayswater and Hyde Park Corner . . .'

Two
'How wonderful,' says White, 'is the economy
of Providence with regard
to the limbs of so vile [sic] a reptile . . .
as soon as the legs sprout
the tail drops off as useless,
and the animal betakes itself to the land.'

Three
But the frog cries thus—Grook Grook Grook.
Or—Quar Quar Quar. (Its nuptial pads shining.)
Or—Oop Oop Oop.
Or—Keck Keck Keck.
Or—Bree ke-ke-ke. (This last is purred.)

The Agile Frog is a poor swimmer,
but on land
capable of very long leaps,
whereas The Painted Frog
is noted for a rather quiet rolling 'laugh'.

Four
The frog
has more enemies than any other Amphibian
in the British Isles. O sadness.
O sad dreams for the frog, with so many enemies.

Five
Frogs prefer lengthy monologues,
not cabaret songs.
They do not paint their faces.
In a fairy tale a frog can do magic things,
and never worries
about the end of the world,
as he dream-dawdles along the wondrous walks
of the wet grass . . .

In the moon's slummocky illumination
he's like a walking prayer . . .

Six
In very rainy times
frogs crowd the suburban lawns
like so many green young Beethovens
chorusing: 'We dream, we dream . . .'

Seven
A frog in a dream
is worth two in the hand.
Do not be my enemy, says dream-frog.

Eight
Here is a painting of a frog
by the artist Watteau,
a frog silkclad amid classical architecture,
plus pond . . .

Here is a frog big as a statue of the Buddha,
gold-leafed and amazing,
eyes yellow as underwater silk . . .

Here is an English frog,
the giant stone Frog of Lanner,
which hops about,
massive, amiable and wise . . .
having defeated all his enemies
by outdreaming them . . .

George Szirtes

THE LUKÁCS BATHS

1

It's circa 1900 and five women
have gathered here in semi-darkness
prepared to prophesy their own extinction.
The water shimmies down a pebbled wall,
a fountain hesitates. Their swimming costumes
are wasps' nests soaked through, softened by the gush,
their bathing caps are a green efflorescence.
They are the light at the bottom of deep pools
wobbling in uncomfortable sunshine
with rheumatic feet, imagining a Greece
ravaged by wars, prepared, they say, to sink.

2

Inside every grandmother there sits
an attractive young girl mouthing pieties,
complaining of sore lips or God knows what.
They prophesy the past with unerring accuracy;
history for them is painful gossip
half way between myth and memory.
They are on nodding terms with skeletons
who take the shape of husbands in dull rooms,
and they can tell the future as it shrinks
into its faint determined pattern.
It's hard to like them, harder to dislike them.
Their faces are light wrinkles in the water.

3

An enormous beech is jutting from the yard,
The walls, just as in crematoriums
are stuck with plaques in a handful of languages.
My shoulder's better. I can move my leg.
God bless these healing waters. I can walk.
Inside and on the roof the swimsuits bulge.
I'm watching two old women as they swim
and push away the past like tired waves.

Andrew Waterman

DORA, DICK, NIP AND FLUFF

Here is Dora. Here is Dick. And here
Is Nip. And here is Fluff. The sun shines clear
From a blue sky. See Nip and Fluff at play.
Nip is black and white. Fluff's fur is grey.
'Woof,' says Nip. Fluff jumps up on the wall.
Here comes Dora with a bouncy ball.
How Nip romps [new word] with it. But now
Dora throws the red ball high. 'Mee-ow,'
Says Fluff, 'I think that this is meant for me.'
And look, the ball is stuck up in a tree.
'Go after it,' says Dora. See Fluff climb
To a high limb [which only *looks* a rhyme].
'Mee-ow,' says Fluff, 'I cannot get the ball.'
'Come down,' calls Dora. 'But I think I'll fall,'
Says Fluff, 'Mee-ow, mee-ow, I can't go down.'
'Oh, poor Fluff,' says Dora with a frown
[New word]. 'Woof, woof,' barks Nip, 'Let us fetch Dick.'
They go indoors, tell Dick. Dick gets a stick.
Dick runs into the garden. 'I can get
Fluff down and the ball too,' he says. 'Poor pet,'
Says Dora. Dick climbs up the tree and takes
Fluff in his arms, pokes with his stick and shakes
Until the ball drops bouncing. Soon he's got
Himself and Fluff down. Dora's so glad. 'What
Shall we play now?' she chuckles, 'Games are fun.'
They chase [new word] each other. See Nip run.
'Dick, your chum Hamie's here, for tea,' calls Mum.

But Shakespeare [new word] knew there's more to come.

I that please some, try all, both joy and terror.
Of good and bad; that makes and unfolds error,
Now take upon me, in the name of Time,
To use my wings. Impute it not a crime
To me, or my swift passage, that I glide
O'er sixteen years, and leave the growth untried…

See Dick, flat out on a soiled mattress, clutch
His head. He has the shakes. Dick drinks too much.
Divorce [new word and new experience]
Has fouled Dick up. 'Thank God I had the sense
Not to have kids,' Dick says. Dick's lost his job.
He puts off girls he chases. Dick's a slob.
He swigs his bedside Scotch. 'I'll make the door.'
Dick trips on something smelly on the floor.
'Grrr.' Yes, it's Nip. Poor Nip can hardly stand.
Nip has the runs. He cannot understand
The new words 'stomach tumour'. Soon he'll die
[New experience], not knowing why.

See Baby Tim clap hands in Dora's face,
Not knowing he's classed as a high risk case
At Social Services. Tim's still too dumb
To ask why Granny's younger than his Mum.
'It's Dad's remarriage to that teenage bitch
Who paints her toenails green,' says Dora, 'which
Made me quit college.' Dora's on the game.
And heroin [no, this word's not the same
as heroine]. Prone as often as her brother
But under some man, each just like another.
'Go after it,' says Dora, to their shoving
Buttocks. She tells Dick, 'I'm just fun-loving.'
See Baby drop his toy car. He says 'Fuck'
[New word], copying Mummy when, her luck
Out, she drops a pan. Tim smiles. All's well.
Mummy doesn't. Some hope. Time will tell.

That's life. Dick's old chum Hamlet's off his head,
Finding his uncle's killed his father to bed
His mum. See Dick fall down in his own sick.

I've not forgotten Fluff, even if Dick
And Dora have. Cats have nine lives, but how
Each flashes past. Fluff would be dead by now.
But sixteen years ago, in fact one day
Later, Fluff met a fox. She tried to play.
'Mee-o' was mown short. See Fluff's flying fur.
It didn't feel so quick a death to her.

For Dick and Dora still what, if they knew it
Was coming at them, neither would go through it.
They do not see yet cancer, madness, heart
Disease; past cure [new experience]; each fresh start
Mocked by its outcome; then the vortex fear
Of age; still worse, what dulls that, close and near.

No fun. Meanwhile, see Dick gazing down
Into the river where the summer town,
Is mirrored, houses, shop-fronts, trees, intact,
Inverted and at peace. Waters refract
To purity the spoiled, soured life we've got.
Dick knows he'd drown there. Wishes he did not.
He thrashes it with a stick, and sets it shaking,
Until the globe of the lost world falls, breaking.

Glyn Wright

The Mary Ellens

They called us the Mary Ellens of the boats,
up and down gangplank with buckets of cold water,
soaping and scrubbing and swilling off; polishing
brasswork till your face looked back we sang:
Vicar oh vicar please stuff your revelations…

Those sea winds whipped our faces raw. Winter nights
your handrag froze. This scouring stuff like gritty acid
near took off skin as we balanced on trestles, sang:
Vicar oh vicar please stuff your revelations
just give us a feller with a dick like a donkey.

We paraded like an aproned army when job was done.
Starched and spotless. Our boss marched decks
like a bowler-hatted general going cross-eyed
staring at his tips, while we whispered at his back:
Fingers like parsnips and a dick like a radish.

I had the cleanest step in our street, but you
couldn't escape dirt: coaldust and carbon black.
You scrubbed your house but bugs hid in the wall.
Only in church, you shut the door on muck and sang:
There is a green hill far away; Jerusalem the Golden.

Kit Wright

THE ALL-PURPOSE COUNTRY & WESTERN SELF-PITY SONG

He jumped off the box-car
In Eastbourne, the beast born
In him was too hungry to hide:

His neck in grief's grommet,
He groaned through his vomit
At the churn
And the yearn
At the turn
Of the tide.

He headed him soon
For a sad-lit saloon
In back of the edge of the strand,
Where a man almost ended
Sat down and extended

His speckled,
Blue-knuckled
And cuckolded
Hand.

Cried, The wind broke my marriage in two.
Clean through the bones of it,
Christ how it blew!
I got no tomorrow
And sorrow
Is tough to rescind:
So forgive me if I should break wind, son,
Forgive me
If I should break wind.

At this the bartender
Addressed the agenda,
A dish-cloth kept dabbing his eye.
Said, Pardon intrusion
Upon your effusion
Of loss but none wooed it
Or rued it
As I.

For after the eve of Yvonne,
My God, how it hurts now the woman has gone!
Heart-sick as a dog,
I roll on like a log
Down the roaring black river
Where once sailed
A swan.

Then the dog on the floor,
Who'd not spoken before,
Growled, Ain't it the truth you guys said?
I may be a son-
Of-a-bitch but that bitch

Was my Sun
And she dumped me,
The bitch did,
For dead.

So three lonely guys in the night and a hound
Drank up, and they headed them out to the Sound,
Threw up, then they threw themselves
In and they
Drowned.

O dee-o-dayee . . .
O dee-o-dayee . . .
Woe-woe-dalayee . . .

Peter Wyton

At the End of the Killing Line

Age: 15. Height: 4'9". Status: executive. Evidence:
tie, shoes, clip-board, nervous tic. Duties: weighing
(in transit, right to left) wheeled vats of kidneys,
hearts, heads, trotters, sweetbreads. (In transit,
left to right) wheeled trolleys, stacked with
shop-bound products. I subtract tare of vehicle
from weight of quivering offal, push periodic slips
through pigeon-hole to super-exec, in portaphonebox
with own stool. View: tiles, hooks, swinging carcasses,
flashing knives. Leisure activities: lunch break soccer
in loading yard with vat and trolley shovers, all twice
my size, clog shod, with socialist principles, or
watching older men play billiards, in a Capstan full
strength cloud, amidst a grunting, coughing scrum.
Places I seldom go, if I can help it: 1. Upstairs,
where there are people in suits. 2. The opposite end
of the killing line, where pigs are individually
stampeded through a channel, underneath a rusted stile,
where the man stands with the fag hanging from his lip,
one eye closed, the long mallet arcing over and down.